Y0-ABJ-033

PRACTICING TO TAKE THE

GRE®

COMPUTER SCIENCE TEST

AN OFFICIAL FULL-LENGTH EDITION OF THE GRE COMPUTER SCIENCE TEST ADMINISTERED IN 1985-86

Published by Educational Testing Service
for the Graduate Record Examinations Board

The Graduate Record Examinations Program offers a General Test measuring verbal, quantitative, and analytical abilities and Subject Tests measuring achievement in the following 17 fields:

Biology	Education	Literature in	Political
Chemistry	Engineering	English	Science
Computer	French	Mathematics	Psychology
Science	Geology	Music	Sociology
Economics	History	Physics	Spanish

The tests are administered by Educational Testing Service under policies determined by the Graduate Record Examinations Board, an independent board affiliated with the Association of Graduate Schools and the Council of Graduate Schools in the United States.

The Graduate Record Examinations Board has officially made available for purchase one full-length edition of each of the following Subject Tests: Biology, Chemistry, Computer Science, Economics, Education, Engineering, History, Literature in English, Physics, and Psychology. Two practice books, each containing three General Tests, are also available. These practice books may be purchased by using the order form on page 55.

Full-length editions of the other Subject Tests, are not yet available. However, individual booklets describing each test and including sample questions and score interpretation information are available free of charge for all 17 Subject Tests. These booklets may be requested by writing to:

Graduate Record Examinations Program
CN 6014
Princeton, NJ 08541-6014

Practicing to Take the GRE® Computer Science Test

This practice book contains the full-length GRE® Computer Science Test that was given at GRE test centers in December 1985. It has been published on behalf of the Graduate Record Examinations Board to help potential graduate students prepare to take the test.

The book includes information about the purpose of the GRE Subject Tests, a detailed description of the content specifications for the GRE Computer Science Test, and the procedures for developing the test. This information also appears in the descriptive booklet you will receive when you register to take the test. The practice book contains a complete test book, including the general instructions printed on the back cover and inside back cover. Before you take the test at the test center, you will be given time to read these instructions. They show you how to mark your answer sheet properly and give you advice about guessing.

Try to take this practice test under conditions that simulate those in an actual test administration. Use the answer sheet provided on pages 53 and 54 and mark your answers with a number 2 (soft-lead) pencil, as you will do at the test center. Give yourself 2 hours and 50 minutes in a quiet place and work through the test without interruption, focusing your attention on the questions with the same concentration you would use in taking the test to earn a score. Since you will not be permitted to use them at the test center, do not use dictionaries or other books, compasses, rulers, slide rules, calculators, calculator/watch combinations, or any other aids.

After you complete the test, use the work sheet and conversion table on pages 6 and 7 to score your test. The work sheet also shows the percentage of those who took the test in December 1985 who answered each question correctly so that you can compare your performance on the questions with theirs. Evaluating your performance on the questions should help you determine whether you would benefit by reviewing certain courses before taking the test at the test center.

We believe that if you use this practice book as we have suggested, you will be able to approach the testing experience with increased confidence.

PURPOSE OF THE GRE SUBJECT TESTS

The GRE Subject Tests are designed to help graduate school committees and fellowship sponsors assess the qualifications of applicants in their respective subject fields. The tests also provide students with a means of assessing their own competence.

Scores on the tests are intended to indicate students' mastery of the subject matter emphasized in many undergraduate programs. Since past achievement is usually a good indicator of future performance, the scores aid in predicting students' probable success in advanced study. Because the tests are standardized, the test scores permit comparison of the competence of students from different institutions with different undergraduate programs.

The Graduate Record Examinations Board recommends that scores on the Subject Tests be evaluated in conjunction with other relevant information about applicants. Because numerous factors influence success in graduate school, reliance on a single measure to predict success is not advisable. Other indicators of competence typically include transcripts showing the range of courses taken and the grades earned, letters of recommendation, and GRE General Test scores.

DEVELOPMENT OF THE COMPUTER SCIENCE TEST

Each new edition of the Computer Science Test is developed by a committee of examiners composed of specialists in various aspects of the field who come from undergraduate and graduate faculties representative of different types of institutions and different regions of the United States. In selecting members of this committee, the GRE Program staff seeks the advice of the Association for Computing Machinery and the Computer Society of the Institute of Electrical and Electronic Engineers.

Subject-matter and measurement specialists on the ETS staff assist the committee of examiners. They provide information and advice about methods of test construction and help prepare the questions and assemble the test.

Because of the diversity of undergraduate curricula in computer science, it is not possible, within the limitations of a test, to cover all the material that examinees may have studied. The examiners, therefore, try to select questions that sample the basic knowledge and understanding most important for successful graduate study in the field. The committee works to keep the test up-to-date. New editions are developed regularly so the test content changes steadily but gradually, much like most curricula. When a new edition is introduced into the program, it is equated; that is, the scores are related to those on previous editions by statistical methods so that scores from all active editions are directly comparable. Although they do not contain the same questions, all editions of the test are constructed according to equivalent specifications for content and level of difficulty and each measures equivalent knowledge and skills.

After a new edition of the Computer Science Test has been taken by examinees at an international test administration, the performance of the examinees on each question is analyzed. If this analysis and the accompanying appraisal of content reveals that a question is not satisfactory—that it is ambiguous or inappropriate for the group taking the test—the answers to that question are not used in computing the scores.

CONTENT OF THE GRE COMPUTER SCIENCE TEST

The test consists of about 80 multiple-choice questions, some of which are grouped in sets and based on such materials as diagrams, graphs, and program fragments.

The approximate distribution of questions in each edition of the test according to content categories is indicated by the following outline. The percentages given are approximate; actual percentages will vary slightly from one edition of the test to another.

I. **SOFTWARE SYSTEMS AND METHODOLOGY—35%**
   A. Data organization
      1. Abstract data types (e.g., stacks, queues, lists, strings, trees, sets)
      2. Implementations of data types (e.g., pointers, hashing, encoding, packing, address arithmetic)
      3. File organization (e.g., sequential, indexed, multilevel)
      4. Data models (e.g., hierarchical, relational, network)
   B. Organization of program control
      1. Iteration and recursion
      2. Functions, procedures, and exception handlers
      3. Concurrent processes, interprocess communication, and synchronization
   C. Programming languages and notation
      1. Applicative *versus* procedural languages
      2. Control and data structure
      3. Scope, extent, and binding
      4. Parameter passing
      5. Expression evaluation
   D. Design and development
      1. Program specification
      2. Development methodologies
      3. Development tools
   E. Systems
      1. Examples (e.g., compilers, operating systems)
      2. Performance models
      3. Resource management (e.g., scheduling, storage allocation)
      4. Protection and security

II. **COMPUTER ORGANIZATION AND ARCHITECTURE—20%**
   A. Logic design
      1. Implementation of combinational and sequential circuits
      2. Functional properties of digital integrated circuits
   B. Processors and control units
      1. Instruction sets, register and ALU organization
      2. Control sequencing, register transfers, microprogramming, pipelining
   C. Memories and their hierarchies
      1. Speed, capacity, cost
      2. Cache, main, secondary storage
      3. Virtual memory, paging, segmentation devices
   D. I/O devices and interfaces
      1. Functional characterization, data rate, synchronizatio
      2. Access mechanism, interrupts
   E. Interconnection
      1. Bus and switch structures
      2. Network principles and protocols
      3. Distributed resources

III. THEORY—20%

A. Automata and language theory
1. Regular languages (e.g., finite automata, nondeterministic finite automata, regular expressions)
2. Context-free languages (e.g., notations for grammars, properties such as emptiness, ambiguity)
3. Special classes of context-free grammars (e.g., LL, LR, precedence)
4. Turing machines and decidability
5. Processors for formal languages (e.g., parsers, parser generators)

B. Correctness of programs
1. Formal specifications and assertions (e.g., pre- and postassertions, loop invariants, invariant relations of a data structure)
2. Verification techniques (e.g., predicate transformers, Hoare axioms)

C. Analysis of algorithms
1. Exact or asymptotic analysis of the best, worst, or average case of the time and space complexity of specific algorithms
2. Upper and lower bounds on the complexity of specific problems
3. NP-completeness

IV. COMPUTATIONAL MATHEMATICS—20%

A. Discrete structures—Basic elements of:
1. Abstract algebra
2. Mathematical logic, including Boolean algebra
3. Combinatorics
4. Graph theory
5. Set theory
6. Discrete probability
7. Recurrence relations

B. Numerical mathematics
1. Computer arithmetic
2. Classical numerical algorithms
3. Linear algebra

V. SPECIAL TOPICS—5%

Typical topics might include modeling and simulation, information retrieval, artificial intelligence, computer graphics, and data communications.

TEST-TAKING STRATEGY

Presumably, if you are about to take the GRE Computer Science Test, you have completed or nearly completed an undergraduate major in that subject. Reviewing your curriculum is probably the best way for you to prepare to take the test. Because the test provides reliable measurement over a broad range of subject matter, you should not expect to be familiar with the content of every question.

When you take the test, read the test directions carefully and work as rapidly as you can without being careless. Do not spend too much time pondering questions you find extremely difficult or unfamiliar because no question carries greater weight than any other.

You receive one "raw score" point for a right answer and nothing for an omission; one-fourth of a point is lost for each wrong answer. As a result of this procedure, random guessing will probably not increase your score, so it is not a useful strategy. However, if you have some knowledge about a question and can eliminate one or more of the answer choices as wrong, your chance of getting the right answer is improved and, on the average, it will be to your advantage to answer the question. Each raw score is converted to a scaled score for reporting.

WORK SHEET for the COMPUTER SCIENCE Test, Form GR8629
Answer Key and Percentage* of Examinees Answering Each Question Correctly

Question Number	Answer	P+	TOTAL R	W
1	D	64		
2	C	22		
3	D	83		
4	B	29		
5	A	44		
6	B	6		
7	D	95		
8	C	69		
9	B	47		
10	C	21		
11	C	52		
12	B	10		
13	B	61		
14	B	39		
15	A	58		
16	A	75		
17	B	54		
18	D	49		
19	E	54		
20	E	41		
21	E	22		
22	C	19		
23	D	15		
24	C	44		
25	B	18		
26	B	19		
27	E	46		
28	A	32		
29	C	47		
30	A	69		
31	C	45		
32	A	60		
33	B	57		
34	C	47		
35	B	62		

Right (R) _____

Wrong (W) _____

Question Number	Answer	P+	TOTAL R	W
36	A	55		
37	D	30		
38	E	29		
39	B	49		
40	D	22		
41	D	9		
42	A	28		
43	C	23		
44	A	46		
45	D	52		
46	B	49		
47	D	10		
48	E	39		
49	A	16		
50	D	40		
51	C	14		
52	B	34		
53	A	16		
54	C	62		
55	D	20		
56	C	83		
57	A	42		
58	E	69		
59	C	21		
60	E	18		
61	D	46		
62	A	18		
63	B	29		
64	D	23		
65	A	31		
66	C	34		
67	C	16		
68	D	67		
69	D	37		
70	E	8		

Right (R) _____

Wrong (W) _____

Question Number	Answer	P+	TOTAL R	W
71	A	21		
72	B	32		
73	E	12		
74	D	13		
75	D	17		
76	C	17		
77	A	6		
78	B	35		
79	C	11		
80	A	27		

Right (R) _____

Wrong (W) _____

Total Score

R − W/4 = _____

Scaled Score (SS) = _____

*Estimated P + for the group of examinees who took the GRE Computer Science Test in a recent three year period.

HOW TO SCORE YOUR TEST

The work sheet on page 6 lists the correct answers to the questions. Columns are provided for you to mark whether you chose the right (R) answer or a wrong (W) answer to each question. Draw a line across any question you omitted, because it is not counted in the scoring. At the bottom of each "total" column, enter the number right and the number wrong. Then add the three column totals across to get the total right and total wrong. Divide the total wrong by 4 and subtract the resulting number from the total right. This is the adjustment made for guessing. Then round the result to the nearest whole number. This will give you your raw total score. Use the total score conversion table below to find the scaled total score that corresponds to your raw total score.

Example: Suppose you chose the right answers to 32 questions and wrong answers to 26. Dividing 26 by 4 yields 6.5. Subtracting 6.5 from 32 equals 25.5, which is rounded to 26. The raw score of 26 corresponds to a scaled score of 630.

SCORE CONVERSIONS AND PERCENTS BELOW*
FOR GRE COMPUTER SCIENCE TEST, Form GR8629

TOTAL SCORE					
Raw Score	Scaled Score	%	Raw Score	Scaled Score	%
79-80	990	99	35	690	79
78	980	99	33-34	680	76
76-77	970	99	32	670	73
75	960	99	31	660	69
73-74	950	99	29-30	650	66
72	940	99	28	640	62
70-71	930	99	26-27	630	58
69	920	99	25	620	55
67-68	910	99	23-24	610	51
66	900	99	22	600	47
64-65	890	99	20-21	590	43
63	880	99	19	580	39
61-62	870	99	17-18	570	35
60	860	99	16	560	32
58-59	850	99	14-15	550	28
57	840	99	13	540	25
56	830	99	11-12	530	22
54-55	820	98	10	520	19
53	810	98	9	510	16
51-52	800	97	7-8	500	14
50	790	96	6	490	11
48-49	780	95	4-5	480	9
47	770	94	3	470	8
45-46	760	93	1-2	460	6
44	750	92	0	450	5
42-43	740	90			
41	730	89			
39-40	720	86			
38	710	84			
36-37	700	81			

*Percent scoring below the scaled score based on the performance of the 11,458 examinees who took the GRE Subject Test in Computer Science between October 1, 1981, and September 30, 1984.

EVALUATING YOUR PERFORMANCE

Now that you have scored your test, you may wish to see how your scores compare with those earned by others who took this test. For this purpose, the performance of a sample of the examinees who took the test in December 1985 was analyzed. The sample was selected to represent the total population of GRE examinees tested between October 1981 and September 1984. Interpretive data based on the scores earned by these examinees are to be used by admissions officers in 1986-87. By comparing your performance on this practice test with the performance of the analysis sample, you will be able to determine your strengths and weaknesses and can then plan a program of study to prepare yourself for taking the Computer Science Test under standard conditions.

Two kinds of information are provided. On the work sheet you used to determine your score is a column labeled "P + ." The numbers in this column indicate the percent of the examinees in the analysis sample who answered each question correctly. In a test of this kind, a question is considered to be of average difficulty if it is answered correctly by about 60 percent (P+ = 60) of the examinees. Use this as a guide for evaluating your performance on the questions that deal with topics covered in the undergraduate courses you have taken. On these questions, you should do relatively well. There are probably some questions on material you have not encountered in your undergraduate program. You may have omitted these questions or guessed at answers, and your performance on them contributes little to your score.

The other kind of information provided is based on the total scores earned by the analysis sample. It appears in the conversion table for total scores in a column to the right of the scaled scores and shows for each total scaled score the percent of the analysis sample who received lower scores. For example, in the percent column opposite the scaled score 550 is the percent 29. This means that 29 percent of the analysis sample examinees scored lower than 550 on this test. Note the percent paired with the total scaled score you made on the practice test. That number is a reasonable indication of your rank among GRE Computer Science Test examinees if you followed the test-taking suggestions in this practice book.

It is important to realize that the conditions under which you tested yourself were not exactly the same as those you will encounter at a test center. It is impossible to predict how differing test-taking conditions will affect test performance, but this is one factor that may account for differences between your practice test scores and your actual test scores.

ADDITIONAL INFORMATION

If you have any questions about any of the information in this book, please write to:

Graduate Record Examinations Program
CN 6000
Princeton, NJ 08541-6000

Before you start timing yourself on the test that follows, we suggest that you remove the answer sheet (page 53) and turn first to the back cover of the test book (page 52), as you will do at the test center, and follow the instructions for completing the identification areas of the answer sheet. Then read the inside back cover instructions (page 51). When you are ready to begin the test, note the time and start marking your answers to the questions on the answer sheet.

FORM GR8629

29

THE GRADUATE RECORD EXAMINATIONS

COMPUTER SCIENCE TEST

*Do not break the seal
until you are told to do so.*

*The contents of this test are confidential.
Disclosure or reproduction of any portion
of it is prohibited.*

COMPUTER SCIENCE TEST

Time—170 minutes

80 Questions

Notation and Conventions:

In this test a reading knowledge of Pascal-like languages is assumed. The following notational conventions are used.

1. All numbers are assumed to be written in decimal notation unless otherwise indicated.

2. $\lfloor x \rfloor$ denotes the greatest integer that is less than or equal to x.

3. $\lceil x \rceil$ denotes the least integer that is greater than or equal to x.

4. $g(n) = O(f(n))$ denotes "$g(n)$ has order $f(n)$" and, for purposes of this test, may be taken to mean that $\lim\limits_{n \to \infty} \left| \dfrac{g(n)}{f(n)} \right|$ is finite.

5. $\exists$ denotes "there exists."

   $\forall$ denotes "for all."

   $\Rightarrow$ denotes "implies."

   $\neg$ denotes "not"; "$\overline{A}$" is also used as meaning "$\neg A$."

   $\vee$ denotes "inclusive or."

   $\oplus$ denotes "exclusive or."

   $\wedge$ denotes "and"; also, juxtaposition of statements denotes "and," e.g., PQ denotes "P and Q".

6. If A and B denote sets, then:

   $A \cup B$ is the set of all elements that are in A or in B or in both;

   $A \cap B$ is the set of all elements that are in both A and B; AB also denotes $A \cap B$;

   $\overline{A}$ is the set of all elements not in A that are in some specified universal set.

7. In a string expression, if S and T denote strings or sets of strings, then:

   An empty string is denoted by ϵ or by Λ;

   ST denotes the concatenation of S and T;

   $S + T$ denotes $S \cup T$ or $\{S, T\}$ depending on context;

   S^n denotes $\underbrace{SS \ldots S}_{n \text{ factors}}$;

   S^* denotes $\epsilon + S + S^2 + S^3 + \ldots$.

GO ON TO THE NEXT PAGE.

8. In a grammar:

$\alpha \longrightarrow \beta$ represents a production in the grammar.

$\alpha \Longrightarrow \beta$ means β can be derived from α by the application of exactly one production.

$\alpha \overset{*}{\Longrightarrow} \beta$ means β can be derived from α by the application of zero or more productions.

Unless otherwise specified

   (i)   symbols appearing on the left-hand side of productions are nonterminal symbols, the remaining symbols are terminal symbols,

   (ii) the leftmost symbol of the first production is the start symbol, and

   (iii) the start symbol is permitted to appear on the right-hand side of productions.

9. In a logic diagram:

represents an AND element.

represents an inclusive OR element.

represents an exclusive OR element.

represents a NOT element.

represents a NAND element.

represents a NOR element.

10. represents a D-type flip-flop, which stores the value of its D input when clocked.

11. Binary tree traversal is defined recursively as follows:

   preorder - visit the root, traverse the left subtree, traverse the right subtree

   inorder   - traverse the left subtree, visit the root, traverse the right subtree

   postorder - traverse the left subtree, traverse the right subtree, visit the root

12. In a finite automaton diagram, states are represented by circles, with final (or accepting) states indicated by two concentric circles. The start state is indicated by the word "Start." An arc from state s to state t labeled a indicates a transition from s to t on input a. A label a/b indicates that this transition produces an output b. A label $a_1, a_2, \ldots, a_k$ indicates that the transition is made on any of the inputs $a_1, a_2, \ldots, a_k$.

GO ON TO THE NEXT PAGE.

Directions: Each of the questions or incomplete statements below is followed by five suggested answers or completions. Select the one that is best and then blacken the corresponding space on the answer sheet.

1. The number of 1's in the binary representation of

$$13*16^3 + 11*16^2 + 9*16 + 3$$

is which of the following?

(A) 7   (B) 8   (C) 9   (D) 10   (E) 12

---

2. Which of the following sorting algorithms has average-case and worst-case running times of $O(n \log n)$?

(A) Bubble sort   (B) Insertion sort   (C) Merge sort   (D) Quicksort   (E) Selection sort

---

3. With regard to the Pascal declarations

     type
        Vector = **array**[1..10] **of** *integer* ;
     var
        a   : *Vector* ;
        b,c   : **array**[1..10] **of** *integer* ;
        d   : *Vector* ;

which of the following is FALSE ?

(A) *a* and *b* have structurally equivalent types.
(B) *a* and *d* have name equivalent types.
(C) *b* and *c* have structurally equivalent types.
(D) *b* and *d* have name equivalent types.
(E) *a*, *c*, and *d* have structurally equivalent types.

GO ON TO THE NEXT PAGE.

4. In the NoNicks operating system, the time required by a single file-read operation has four <u>nonoverlapping</u> components:

> disk seek time—25 msec
> disk latency time—8 msec
> disk transfer time—1 msec per 1,000 bytes
> operating system overhead—1 msec per 1,000 bytes + 10 msec

In version 1 of the system, the file read retrieved blocks of 1,000 bytes. In version 2, the file read (along with the underlying layout on disk) was modified to retrieve blocks of 4,000 bytes. The ratio of the time required to read a large file under version 2 to the time required to read the same large file under version 1 is approximately

(A) 1:4   (B) 1:3.5   (C) 1:1   (D) 1.1:1   (E) 2.7:1

---

5. Sometimes the object module produced by a compiler includes information (from the symbol table) mapping all source program names to their addresses. The most likely purpose of this information is

(A) for use as input to a debugging aid
(B) to increase the run-time efficiency of the program
(C) for the reduction of the symbol-table space needed by the compiler
(D) to tell the loader where each variable belongs
(E) to tell the operating system what to call the variables

6.

A	B	C	f
0	0	0	1
0	0	1	1
0	1	0	1
0	1	1	x
1	0	0	1
1	0	1	0
1	1	0	1
1	1	1	x

Consider the logic function in the table above, where x denotes a *don't-care* value. Which of the following statements describes correctly the relation between the minimal sum and the minimal product form of f?

(A) They are logically equivalent by definition.
(B) They are logically equivalent because *don't care*'s are used in the same way.
(C) They are logically equivalent because *don't care*'s do not matter.
(D) They are logically not equivalent by definition.
(E) They are logically not equivalent because *don't care*'s are used in different ways.

GO ON TO THE NEXT PAGE.

Questions 7-8 are based on the following program fragment written in a Pascal-like language.

$L1$: **begin**

    var a, b, c : *integer* ;   (1)

    var d, e : *real* ;

    ———
    ———
    ———

$L2$: **begin**

    var a, f : *integer* ;

    var g, h : *real* ;

    ———
    ———
    ———

    end ;

end

Let the designation "block Li" refer to all the statements from the **begin** labeled with Li to its corresponding **end**.

7. In block $L2$ the variables g and h are best described as

(A) dummy variables   (B) parameter variables   (C) global variables

(D) local variables   (E) recursive variables

8. If the notation $L1$-$L2$ means "the portion of block $L1$ that is not in block $L2$," then the scopes of the variables a and b declared in the statement numbered (1) are

(A) $L1$ for a and $L1$ for b (B) $L1$ for a and $L1$-$L2$ for b (C) $L1$-$L2$ for a and $L1$ for b

(D) $L1$-$L2$ for a and $L1$-$L2$ for b (E) $L2$ for a and $L2$ for b

GO ON TO THE NEXT PAGE.

9. The binary relation on the integers defined by

$$R = \{(x, y) : |y - x| \leq 1\}$$

has which of the following properties?

    I.   Reflexivity
   II. Symmetry
  III. Transitivity

(A) None   (B) I and II only   (C) I and III only   (D) II and III only   (E) I, II, and III

---

10. A major advantage of direct mapping of a cache is its simplicity. The main disadvantage of this organization is that

(A) it does not allow simultaneous access to the intended data and its tag
(B) it is more expensive than other types of cache organizations
(C) the cache hit ratio is degraded if two or more blocks used alternately map onto the same block frame in the cache
(D) its access time is greater than that of other cache organizations
(E) the number of blocks required for the cache increases linearly with the size of the main memory

---

11. Two computers communicate with each other by sending data packets across a local area network. The size of these packets is 1,000 bytes. The network has the capacity to carry 1,000 packets per second. The CPU time required to execute the network protocol to send one packet is 10 milliseconds. The maximum rate at which one computer can send data to another is approximately

(A)   10,000 bytes/second
(B)   25,000 bytes/second
(C)   100,000 bytes/second
(D)   500,000 bytes/second
(E) 1,000,000 bytes/second

---

12. The language $\{ww \,|\, w \in (0 + 1)^*\}$ is

(A) not accepted by any Turing machine
(B) accepted by some Turing machine, but by no pushdown automaton
(C) accepted by some pushdown automaton, but not context-free
(D) context-free, but not regular
(E) regular

GO ON TO THE NEXT PAGE.

13. A singly linked list is implemented in two arrays, *VALUE* and *LINK*, in which $LINK[I]$ points to the successor of $VALUE[I]$. If an element not initially in the list is assigned to $VALUE[J]$, then the program fragment

$$LINK[J] := LINK[I] ;$$
$$LINK[I] := J ;$$

is one that

(A) inserts $VALUE[J]$ before $VALUE[I]$ in the list
(B) inserts $VALUE[J]$ after $VALUE[I]$ in the list
(C) replaces $VALUE[J]$ by $VALUE[I]$ in the list
(D) replaces $VALUE[I]$ by $VALUE[J]$ in the list
(E) does none of the above

---

14. Consider the part of the two-dimensional integer grid bounded by point $A = (0, 0)$ at the "southwest" corner and by point $B = (n, n)$ at the "northeast" corner. How many different ways are there of walking from A to B on grid lines, always moving between any two grid points either east or north?

(A) 2^{2n} (B) $\binom{2n}{n}$ (C) $n!$ (D) n^2 (E) $n(n+1)/2$

---

15. Consider the following program fragment.

(1)   **for** $i := 1$ **to** n **do**

(2) $M[i] := 0$

Let A represent the initialization ($i := 1$) in line (1) ; let B represent the "body" of the loop; i.e., line (2). Let I represent the incrementation of i by 1 implied by line (1), and let T represent the test for $i \le n$ also implied by line (1).

Which of the following regular expressions represents all possible sequences of steps taken during execution of the fragment, if it is assumed that n is arbitrary and that no abnormal terminations of the loop can occur?

(A) $AT(BIT)^*$ (B) $A(ITB)^*T$ (C) $AT^*B^*I^*T$ (D) $(ABIT)^*$ (E) $A(TBI)^*$

GO ON TO THE NEXT PAGE.

16. The following iteration, where *I* and *N* have type integer and the value of *I* is unimportant after the iteration,

$I := N$;

while $I > 1$ **do**

    begin

        writeln('hello') ;

        $I := I - 1$

    end

is to be replaced by a call *Foobar*(*N*), where *Foobar* is defined by

procedure *Foobar*(*J* : *integer*) ;

  begin

    BODY

  end ;

A correct value for *BODY* is

(A) **if** $J > 1$ **then**

    begin

      writeln('hello') ;

      Foobar(*J*−1)

    end

(B) *Foobar*(*J*−1) ;

    if $J > 1$ **then**

      writeln('hello')

(C) *Foobar*(*J*−1) ;

    if $J >= 1$ **then**

      writeln('hello')

(D) **if** $J >= 1$ **then**

    begin

      Foobar(*J*−1) ;

      writeln('hello')

    end

(E) **if** $J > 1$ **then**

    writeln('hello') ;

    Foobar(*J*−1)

GO ON TO THE NEXT PAGE.

17.

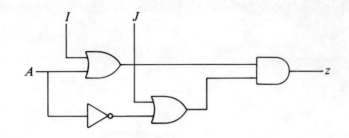

The circuit above is to be used to implement the function $z = f(A,B) = \bar{A} + B$. Inputs I and J can be selected from the set $\{0,1,B,\bar{B}\}$. What values should be chosen for I and J?

(A) $I = 0, J = B$ (B) $I = 1, J = B$ (C) $I = B, J = 1$ (D) $I = \bar{B}, J = 0$ (E) $I = 1, J = \bar{B}$

18.

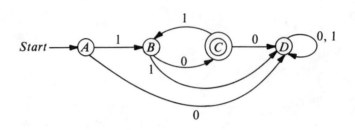

In the figure above, a finite automaton M has start state A and accepting state C. Which of the following regular expressions denotes the set of words accepted by M?

(A) 10^* (B) $(10)^*$ (C) 10^*1^*0 (D) $1(01)^*0$ (E) $(01)^*01$

---

19. A 0-2 binary tree is a rooted tree such that every node has either no child or two children. The height of a binary tree is the maximum number of edges on a path from the root to a leaf. Let $n(h)$ be the minimum number of nodes in a 0-2 binary tree of height h, and let $N(h)$ be the maximum number. For all $h > 0$, $(n(h), N(h)) =$

(A) $(h + 1, 2^h - 1)$ (B) $(h + 1, 2^{h+1})$ (C) $(h + 1, 2^{h+1} - 1)$

(D) $(2h + 1, 2^h - 1)$ (E) $(2h + 1, 2^{h+1} - 1)$

GO ON TO THE NEXT PAGE.

20. Which of the regular expressions below describes the same set of strings as the following grammar (with root S)?

$$S \longrightarrow Ax \quad | \quad By$$
$$A \longrightarrow y \quad | \quad Ay$$
$$B \longrightarrow x \quad | \quad y$$

(A) y*x + xy + y   (B) y*x + x + yy   (C) yy*x + xy + y

(D) y*x + xy + yy   (E) yy*x + xy + yy

---

21. Let A be an $n \times n$ matrix and let P be an $n \times n$ permutation matrix. Which of the following must be true?

(A) $A = P^{-1}AP$ (B) $PA = P(P^{-1}AP)$ (C) $PAP^{-1} = P(P^{-1}AP)P^{-1}$

(D) $AP = (P^{-1}AP)P$ (E) $\det(A) = \det(P^{-1}AP)$

Questions 22-23 are concerned with a single-surface disk drive having the following characteristics.

Number of tracks per disk:	35
Number of sectors per track:	10
Bits per second transfer rate:	250,000
Revolutions per minute rotational speed:	300

Assume that one byte is 8 bits.

22. If no gaps or special formatting is assumed, then the nominal storage capacity, in bytes, of one such disk is

(A) 6,250   (B) 29,267   (C) 218,750   (D) 1,750,000

(E) none of the above

23. Assume that data transfers between the disk and the memory of a host system are interrupt-driven, one byte at a time. If the instructions to accomplish a one-byte transfer take $8\,\mu s$ and the interrupt overhead is $10\,\mu s$, then the time available, in μs, for other computing between byte transfers is

(A) 0   (B) 8   (C) 10   (D) 14   (E) 32

GO ON TO THE NEXT PAGE.

24. Consider a floating-point number system used by a modern computer for solving large numerical problems. Let $\oplus$ denote the floating-point addition in this system. Which of the following statements is true about this system?

(A) If x and y are real numbers with floating-point representations x' and y', respectively, then $x' \oplus y'$ is always the floating-point representation of $x + y$.

(B) The associative law is valid for $\oplus$; i.e.,

$$(u \oplus v) \oplus w = u \oplus (v \oplus w).$$

(C) There are only finitely many floating-point numbers.

(D) The floating-point numbers are equally spaced throughout their range.

(E) None of the above

Questions 25-26 are based on the following information.

In the microprogrammed control unit of the Cucumber-XMP computer, the output of the control store is loaded into a control register. The control store may be addressed from any of three sources: (i) the output of a micro-program counter for sequential access of microinstructions; (ii) a field in the control register to effect a branch microinstruction; (iii) an additional input to which are connected signals derived from other parts of the Cucumber.

25. The additional input is LEAST likely to be used for signals derived from the

(A) CPU instruction opcode
(B) CPU instruction address
(C) CPU instruction addressing mode bits
(D) arithmetic logic unit condition codes
(E) interrupts and/or other types of exception

26. Suppose that the same clock signal is used to increment the microprogram counter and to load the control register. Which of the following assertions is (are) true?

I. Microinstruction execution time is at least two clock periods.
II. Microinstruction execution can be overlapped with fetching the next microinstruction.
III. Unconditional branch microinstructions must necessarily take longer than other types.

(A) I only   (B) II only   (C) III only   (D) I and III   (E) II and III

GO ON TO THE NEXT PAGE.

27. Consider the representation of six-bit numbers by two's complement, one's complement, or by sign and magnitude. In which representation is there overflow from the addition of the integers 011000 and 011000 ?

   (A) Two's complement only
   (B) Sign and magnitude and one's complement only
   (C) Two's complement and one's complement only
   (D) Two's complement and sign and magnitude only
   (E) All three representations

28.

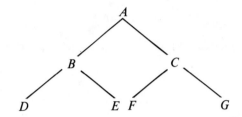

```
init(Q) ;
enqueue(Q,Root) ;
while not empty(Q) do
    begin
        dequeue(Q,a) ;
        if a < > nil then
            begin
                print(a) ;
                enqueue(Q,a↑.left) ;
                enqueue(Q,a↑.right)
            end
    end
```

If the algorithm above is applied to the tree in the figure, which of the following is the output?

   (A) ABCDEFG   (B) ABDECFG   (C) DBEAFCG   (D) DEBFGCA   (E) GFEDCBA

GO ON TO THE NEXT PAGE.

29.

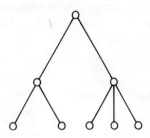

A 2-3 tree is a tree in which

   (i)   every interior node has two or three children, and

   (ii) all paths from the root to a leaf have the same length.

An example of a 2-3 tree is shown above. Which of the following could be the number of interior nodes of a 2-3 tree with 9 leaves?

(A) 5   (B) 6   (C) 7   (D) 8   (E) 9

---

30. Suppose there is an open (external) hash table with four buckets, numbered 0,1,2,3, and integers are hashed into these buckets using hash function $h(x) = x$ mod 4. If the sequence of perfect squares $1, 4, 9, \ldots, i^2, \ldots$ is hashed into the table, then, as the total number of entries in the table grows, what will happen?

(A) Two of the buckets will each get approximately half the entries, and the other two will remain empty.
(B) All buckets will receive approximately the same number of entries.
(C) All entries will go into one particular bucket.
(D) All buckets will receive entries, but the difference between the buckets with smallest and largest number of entries will grow.
(E) Three of the buckets will each get approximately one-third of the entries, and the fourth bucket will remain empty.

GO ON TO THE NEXT PAGE.

31. Consider the following program segment for finding the minimum value of an array.

```
var
    i,j : integer ;
     a : array[1..N] of real ;
begin
    j := 1 ;
    for i := 2 to N do
        if a[i] < a[j] then
            j := i
end
```

Which of the following conditions is (are) true each time the condition of the **if-then** statement is tested?

I. $2 \leq i \leq N$

II. $a[j] \leq a[k]$ for all k such that $1 \leq k < i.$

III. $a[j] \leq a[k]$ for all k such that $2 \leq k \leq i.$

(A) I only   (B) II only   (C) I and II only   (D) I and III only   (E) I, II, and III

---

32. Let the syntactic category $<S>$ be defined by the Backus-Naur form description:

$$<S> ::= r \ell \,|\, r <S> \ell \,|\, <S><S>$$

Which of the following strings can be generated from $<S>$ according to this definition?

I. rr ℓ ℓ r ℓ

II. r ℓ ℓ rrr ℓ ℓ

III. rr ℓ r ℓ r ℓ ℓ r ℓ rr ℓ

(A) I only   (B) II only   (C) III only   (D) I and III   (E) II and III

GO ON TO THE NEXT PAGE.

Questions 33-34 are based on the following code segment that was intended to insert an item into a linked list with ascending keys.

```
type
    List = ↑Node ;
    Node = record
                Data : integer ;
                Next : List
            end ;

var
    p, q, Head : List ;
    Key        : integer ;
    .
    .
    .

    p := Head ;
    if p <> nil then
        while p↑.Data < Key do
            p := p↑.Next ;

    new(q) ;
    q↑.Data := Key ;
    q↑.Next := p↑.Next ;
    p↑.Next := q
```

33. When the segment is executed with a value for *Key* that does <u>not</u> match any value in the list, but is smaller than some value in the list, what happens?

    (A) The new node gets inserted in the correct place.
    (B) The new node gets inserted after the node that it should precede in the list.
    (C) The new node gets inserted before the node that it should follow in the list.
    (D) The new node does not appear in the resulting list.
    (E) The list structure is destroyed.

34. Which of the following is (are) true?

    I.   If the list is nonempty and $Key > n.Data$ for all nodes n in the list, then the code segment will attempt to follow a nil pointer.

    II. If $Head = $ **nil** (indicating an empty list), then after executing the segment *Head* will point to a record containing *Key*.

    III. If $Key = n.Data$ for some node n in the list, then a duplicate will be inserted.

    (A) I only   (B) I and II only   (C) I and III only   (D) II and III only   (E) I, II, and III

GO ON TO THE NEXT PAGE.

35. Two single-user workstations are attached to the same local area network. On one of these workstations, file pages are accessed over the network from a file server; the average access time per page is 0.1 second. On the other of these workstations, file pages are accessed from a local disk; the average access time per page is 0.05 second.

A particular compilation requires 30 seconds of computation and 200 file page accesses. What is the ratio of the total time required by this compilation if run on the diskless (file server) workstation to the total time required if run on the workstation with the local disk, if it is assumed that computation is not overlapped with file access?

(A) 1/1 (B) 5/4 (C) 5/3 (D) 10/5 (E) 3/1

---

36. Consider N employee records to be stored in memory for on-line retrieval. Each employee record is uniquely identified by a social security number. Consider the following ways to store the N records.

   I.   An array sorted by social security number
   II. A linked list sorted by social security number
   III. A linked list not sorted
   IV. A balanced binary search tree with social security number as key

For the structures I-IV, respectively, the average time for an efficient program to find an employee record, given the social security number as key, is which of the following?

	I	II	III	IV
(A)	$O(\log N)$	$O(N)$	$O(N)$	$O(\log N)$
(B)	$O(N)$	$O(\log N)$	$O(N)$	$O(N)$
(C)	$O(\log N)$	$O(\log N)$	$O(N)$	$O(1)$
(D)	$O(N)$	$O(N)$	$O(N)$	$O(1)$
(E)	$O(N)$	$O(\log N)$	$O(\log N)$	$O(1)$

---

37. In a height-balanced binary search tree, the heights of the left and right descendents of any node differ by at most 1. Which of the following are true of such a tree?

   I.   Worst-case search time is logarithmic in the number of nodes.
   II. Average-case search time is logarithmic in the number of nodes.
   III. Best-case search time is proportional to the height of the tree.
   IV. The height of the tree is logarithmic in the number of nodes.

(A) I and III only   (B) II and III only   (C) II and IV only
(D) I, II, and IV   (E) I, III, and IV

GO ON TO THE NEXT PAGE.

38. Three common operations on the symbol table of a compiler are:

    Insert — insert an identifier and its attributes

    Find   — return the attributes of a particular identifier

    List   — list all identifiers and their attributes in lexicographic order

A particular compiler maintains its symbol table as a hash table with $2n$ buckets. For a symbol table with approximately n identifiers, which of the following gives the order of the average cost of efficient programs performing these three operations?

	Insert	*Find*	*List*
(A)	$O(n)$	$O(n)$	$O(n)$
(B)	$O(\log n)$	$O(n)$	$O(n \log n)$
(C)	$O(\log n)$	$O(\log n)$	$O(n)$
(D)	$O(1)$	$O(\log n)$	$O(n)$
(E)	$O(1)$	$O(1)$	$O(n \log n)$

---

39. A 10-unit heap of memory uses an allocation algorithm in which a block is allocated at the left end of the leftmost block in which it fits. Which of the following allocation/deallocation patterns CANNOT be satisfied?

(A) $x := alloc(10)$; $free(x)$; $y := alloc(3)$

(B) $x := alloc(5)$; $y := alloc(3)$; $free(x)$; $z := alloc(6)$

(C) $x := alloc(1)$; $free(x)$; $x := alloc(6)$; $y := alloc(4)$

(D) $x := alloc(9)$; $y := alloc(1)$; $free(x)$; $z := alloc(8)$; $w := alloc(1)$

(E) $x := alloc(5)$; $y := alloc(1)$; $free(x)$; $z := alloc(3)$; $w := alloc(4)$; $v := alloc(2)$

---

40. As $n \to \infty$, the function $2^{\sqrt{n}}$ grows faster than

(A) $\log n$, but slower than $\sqrt{n}$

(B) $\sqrt{n}$, but slower than n

(C) n, but slower than n^2

(D) n^2, but slower than $\sqrt{2^n}$

(E) $\sqrt{2^n}$, but slower than 2^n

GO ON TO THE NEXT PAGE.

41. The bits in the 32-bit word of a hypothetical computer are denoted by:

$$b_{31}b_{30}\ldots b_1 b_0$$

When such a word represents a nonzero floating-point number, its value is taken to be

$$\left(\frac{1}{2} - b_{31}\right)\left(1 + \sum_{i=0}^{23} 2^{i-24} b_i\right) 2^s$$

where $s = -64 + \sum_{i=24}^{30} 2^{i-24} b_i$.

The correct values for the least positive and greatest positive numbers, respectively, that can be represented are given by which of the following pairs?

(A) $2^{-63}, (1 - 2^{-25})2^{64}$

(B) $2^{-64}, (1 - 2^{-24})2^{63}$

(C) $2^{-64}, 2^{63} - 1$

(D) $2^{-65}, (1 - 2^{-25})2^{63}$

(E) $2^{-65}, 2^{64} - 1$

GO ON TO THE NEXT PAGE.

42. In the following program segment, assume that when execution of the segment begins,
$m \leq n$ and $a[m-1] \leq v \leq a[n+1]$.

```
i := m - 1 ;
j := n + 1 ;
while  i < j  do
   begin
      repeat
         i := i + 1
      until  a[i] ≥ v ;

      repeat
         j := j - 1
      until  a[j] ≤ v ;

      if  i < j  then
         begin
            Temp := a[i] ;
            a[i] := a[j] ;
            a[j] := Temp
         end
   end
```

For large values of $n-m$, which of the following best approximates the sum of the number of times the assignments $i := i + 1$ and $j := j - 1$ are executed?

(A) $n-m$

(B) $2(n-m)$

(C) $(n-m)^2$

(D) $(n-m)^2 / 2$

(E) $(n-m)(n-m+1) / 2$

GO ON TO THE NEXT PAGE.

43. If A and B are floating-point numbers stored with 10-bit mantissas and if $A = 1.0$ and $B = 2^{-10}$, which of the following is(are) true?

    I. $A = A + B$
    II. $B = A * B$
    III. $(A + B) + B = A + (B + B)$

(A) I only
(B) III only
(C) I and II only
(D) II and III only
(E) I, II, and III

---

44. The figure below shows a control circuit, consisting of a 3-bit register and some combinational logic. This circuit is initially in the state $Q_1 Q_2 Q_3 = 000$. On subsequent clock pulses, the circuit is required to generate the control sequence: $(100) \rightarrow (010) \rightarrow (001) \rightarrow (001) \rightarrow (001) \rightarrow \ldots$

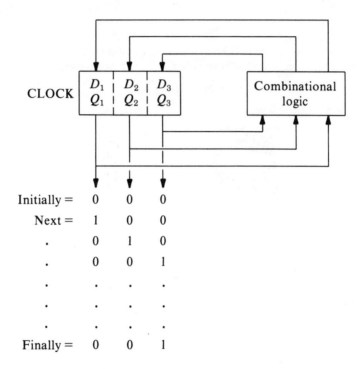

Which of the following is a correct set of equations to be implemented by the combinational logic?

(A) $D_1 = \bar{Q}_1 \bar{Q}_2 \bar{Q}_3,\ D_2 = Q_1\quad\quad,\ D_3 = Q_2 \vee Q_3$
(B) $D_1 = \bar{Q}_1 \bar{Q}_2 \bar{Q}_3,\ D_2 = Q_1 \bar{Q}_2 \bar{Q}_3\ ,\ D_3 = \bar{Q}_1 Q_2 \bar{Q}_3$
(C) $D_1 = \bar{Q}_1\quad\quad\ ,\ D_2 = \bar{Q}_2\quad\quad,\ D_3 = \bar{Q}_3$
(D) $D_1 = \bar{Q}_1 \bar{Q}_2\quad,\ D_2 = \bar{Q}_2 \bar{Q}_3\quad,\ D_3 = \bar{Q}_3 \bar{Q}_1$
(E) $D_1 = Q_3\quad\quad\ ,\ D_2 = Q_1\quad\quad,\ D_3 = Q_2$

GO ON TO THE NEXT PAGE.

Questions 45-46 are based on the following information.

A monochrome bitmap display treats the screen as a rectangular array of pixels (small dots). One bit of memory is associated with each pixel. A pixel is displayed in black if the associated bit is 1, white if it is 0.

The basic operation on such a display causes each bit in a rectangle, *Destination*, to be replaced by the result obtained by applying a Boolean operation to this bit and the corresponding bit in another rectangle, *Source*. (Assume that *Source* and *Destination* are of identical dimensions and nonoverlapping.) There are 16 possible operations corresponding to the 16 possible truth tables of the form:

		Destination	
		0 (white)	1 (black)
Source	0 (white)	W	X
	1 (black)	Y	Z

For example, *X* is the Boolean value that will be assigned to any bit in *Destination* that has an original value of 1 and that has a corresponding bit in *Source* whose value is 0. Let *Source* and *Destination* be as follows.

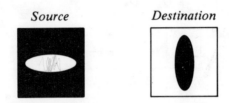

Source   Destination

GO ON TO THE NEXT PAGE.

45. The operation $W=0$ $X=1$ applied to *Source* and *Destination* would yield which of the

                          $Y=1$ $Z=1$

following results?

(A)   (B)   (C)   (D)   (E)

46. What set of values

     W X

     Y Z

would yield the result

when applied to *Source* and *Destination* as given?

(A)	0 0	(B)	1 0	(C)	1 1	(D)	1 1	(E)	0 1
	0 1		0 1		0 0		0 1		0 0

GO ON TO THE NEXT PAGE.

47. Two expressions E and F are said to be <u>unifiable</u> if there are substitutions for the variables of E and F that make the expressions lexically identical. In the following three expressions, only w, x, y, and z are variables.

    I. $f(w,w)$
   II. $f(x,1)$
  III. $f(y,g(z))$

Which pairs of these expressions is(are) pairs of unifiable expressions?

(A) (I, II) only
(B) (I, III) only
(C) (II, III) only
(D) (I, II) and (I, III) only
(E) (I, II), (I, III), and (II, III)

---

48. Several concurrent processes are attempting to share an I/0 device. In an attempt to achieve mutual exclusion, each process is given the following structure. (*Busy* is a shared Boolean variable.)

    $<$ code unrelated to device use $>$

    repeat
    until *Busy* $= false$;

    Busy $:= true$;

    $<$ code to access shared device $>$

    Busy $:= false$;

    $<$ code unrelated to device use $>$

Which of the following is(are) true of this approach?

    I.   It provides a reasonable solution to the problem of guaranteeing mutual exclusion.
   II. It may consume substantial CPU time accessing the *Busy* variable.
  III. It will fail to guarantee mutual exclusion.

(A) I only   (B) II only   (C) III only   (D) I and II   (E) II and III

GO ON TO THE NEXT PAGE.

49. A common method of generating random numbers on a computer is by the method of linear congruential generators:

Choose x_0 (*integer*)

$x_{i+1} = (ax_i + b) \bmod m$ for $i = 0, 1, 2, \ldots,$ where a, b, and m are positive integers.

The period P of the sequence generated by a linear congruential generator is the least positive value of p such that $x_{i+p} = x_i$ for all i. Which of the following is true?

(A) $P \leq m$ for any a, b, x_0.
(B) P may be as large as 2^m for some a, b, x_0.
(C) For any given m and x_0, P is independent of a and b.
(D) For all combinations of a, b, and m, P is independent of x_0.
(E) None of the above

---

50. The construct

cobegin *Statement1* ; *Statement2* **coend**

means *Statement1* and *Statement2* are to be executed in parallel. The only two atomic actions in this construct are loading the value of a variable and storing into a variable. For the program segment

```
x := 0 ;
y := 0 ;
cobegin
  begin
    x := 1 ;
    y := y + x
  end ;
  begin
    y := 2 ;
    x := x + 3
  end
coend
```

which of the following indicate(s) possible values for the variables when the segment finishes execution?

   I. $x = 1$, $y = 2$
  II. $x = 1$, $y = 3$
 III. $x = 4$, $y = 6$

(A) I only
(B) I and II only
(C) I and III only
(D) II and III only
(E) I, II, and III

GO ON TO THE NEXT PAGE.

51. Let L_n be the set of integer points (i,j) in the plane satisfying

$$i, j \text{ integer,}$$
$$i \geqq 0,$$
$$j \geqq 0,$$
$$i+j \leqq n.$$

L_3 is shown below.

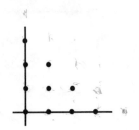

2, 3, 4, 5, 7, 8

The neighborhood $N_n(i,j)$ of point (i,j) in L_n is all those points (k,m) whose coordinates differ, respectively, from those of (i,j) by at most 1; i.e., $N_n(i,j) = \{ (k,m) \in L_n : \ |i-k| \leqq 1 \text{ and } |j-m| \leqq 1\}$. For different (i,j) in L_n, $N_n(i,j)$ may have different sizes. For $n > 3$, the number of different values that can be the size of $N_n(i,j)$ for some $(i,j) \in L_n$ is

(A) 4   (B) 5   (C) 6   (D) 7   (E) 8

52.

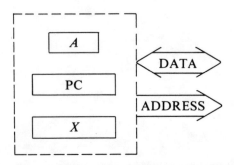

A hypothetical microprocessor communicates with its memory and peripherals over an 8-bit data bus and a 16-bit address bus. It contains an 8-bit accumulator A and two 16-bit registers: program counter PC and index register X. (see diagram above.) The opcode of each instruction is one byte (8 bits) long. Assume that any internal processor time is negligible and that the time to address memory and transfer one byte in either direction over the data bus equals unity (one memory cycle).

The time taken to fetch and execute the 3-byte instruction "store A in some address indexed by X" is

(A) 3   (B) 4   (C) 5   (D) 6   (E) 7

GO ON TO THE NEXT PAGE.

53. The following algorithm solves a system of equations $Lx = b$ where L is a unit lower-triangular matrix (ones on the diagonal and zeros above the diagonal).

```
for i := 1 to n do
  x[i] := b[i] ;
for i := 2 to n do
  for j := 1 to i − 1 do
    < statement >
```

The missing $<$ statement $>$ in the algorithm above is

(A) $x[i] := x[i] − L[i,j]*x[j]$

(B) $x[j] := x[j] − L[i,j]*x[i]$

(C) $x[j] := x[j] − L[i,j]*x[j]$

(D) $x[i] := b[j] − L[i,j]*x[i]$

(E) $x[i] := x[i] − L[i,j]*x[i]$

---

54. A lexical analyzer for Pascal scans the input character-by-character, from a beginning point p until it knows what token begins at p. Assume that the tokens of Pascal are the usual ones: identifiers, constants, keywords, and operators. Sometimes the lexical analyzer must scan beyond the token that begins at p in order to determine what that token is. For which of the following character strings can a lexical analyzer for Pascal determine, without looking at the next character, that it has seen the complete token?

  I. then
  II. <
  III. ;

(A) None   (B) I only   (C) III only   (D) I and II   (E) II and III

GO ON TO THE NEXT PAGE.

55. The following syntax-directed translation scheme is used with a shift-reduce (bottom-up) parser that performs the action in braces immediately after any reduction by the corresponding production.

$A \rightarrow aB$ {print "0"}

$A \rightarrow c$ {print "1"}

$B \rightarrow Ab$ {print "2"}

The string printed when the parser input is aacbb is

(A) 00122   (B) 02021   (C) 10202   (D) 12020   (E) 22100

---

56. For procedures *P1*, *P2*, *P3*, and for Boolean variable *B*, the repeat loop

    P1 ;
    repeat
      P2
    until *B* ;
    P3

is sometimes incorrectly transformed to

  (i)   *P1* ;
 (ii)   **while not** *B* **do**
(iii)   *P2* ;
(iv)   *P3*

The correct version of this transformation is obtained from the incorrect result above by

(A) replacing "**not** *B*" with "*B*" in line (ii)
(B) moving line (i) to between lines (ii) and (iii)
(C) adding a copy of line (iii) between lines (i) and (ii)
(D) adding a copy of line (iv) between lines (ii) and (iii)
(E) replacing "*P1*" by "**if** *B* **then** *P1*"

GO ON TO THE NEXT PAGE.

57. Two 16-bit integers in two's-complement representation, $A = [A_1, A_2, ..., A_{16}]$ and $B = [B_1, B_2, ..., B_{16}]$, where A_1 and B_1 are the sign bits, are added yielding a sum $S = [S_1, S_2, ..., S_{16}]$. A Boolean expression indicating addition overflow is

(A) $S_1 \bar{A}_1 \bar{B}_1 \lor \bar{S}_1 A_1 B_1$

(B) $S_1 A_1 B_1 \lor \bar{S}_1 \bar{A}_1 \bar{B}_1$

(C) $A_1 B_1$

(D) $A_1 B_1 \lor \bar{A}_1 \bar{B}_1$

(E) $A_1 \bar{B}_1 \lor \bar{A}_1 B_1$

---

58. A stack can be defined abstractly by the following rules. Let s be a stack, and let X be a symbol. Then:

(1) ϵ, the "empty stack," is a stack.

(2) $PUSH(s, X)$ is a stack.

(3) $POP(PUSH(s, X)) = s$

(4) $TOP(PUSH(s, X)) = X$

For example:

$TOP(POP(PUSH(PUSH(\epsilon, X), Y)))$

$= TOP(PUSH(\epsilon, X))$ [rule 3 with $s = PUSH(\epsilon, X)$]

$= X$ [rule 4 with $s = \epsilon$]

All of the following are derivable from statements (1), (2), (3), and (4) EXCEPT:

(A) $TOP(PUSH(PUSH(\epsilon, X), Y)) = Y$

(B) $POP(PUSH(\epsilon, X)) = \epsilon$

(C) $PUSH(POP(PUSH(\epsilon, X)), Y)$ is a stack.

(D) $TOP(PUSH(POP(PUSH(\epsilon, X)), Y)) = Y$

(E) $POP(POP(PUSH(\epsilon, X))) = X$

GO ON TO THE NEXT PAGE.

59. For $x \geqq 0$, $y \geqq 0$, define $A(x, y)$ by

$$A(0, y) = y + 1,$$
$$A(x + 1, 0) = A(x, 1), \text{ and}$$
$$A(x + 1, y + 1) = A(x, A(x + 1, y)).$$

Then, for all non-negative integers y, $A(1, y)$ is

(A) 2
(B) $y + 1$
(C) $y + 2$
(D) $2y + 3$
(E) none of the above

---

60. If L is a language accepted by some automaton M, which of the following is(are) true?

    I. If M is a nondeterministic finite automaton, then L is accepted by some deterministic finite automaton.
    II. If M is a deterministic pushdown automaton, then L is accepted by some nondeterministic pushdown automaton.
    III. If M is a nondeterministic pushdown automaton, then L is accepted by some deterministic Turing machine.

(A) I only   (B) III only   (C) I and II only   (D) II and III only   (E) I, II, and III

GO ON TO THE NEXT PAGE.

Questions 61-62 are based on the following program segment.

```
for Pass := 1 to N−1 do
  begin
    for Item := 1 to N − Pass do
      begin
        if List[Item] < List[Item+1] then
          begin
            Temp := List[Item] ;
            List[Item] := List[Item+1] ;
            List[Item+1] := Temp
          end
      end
    (* 1 *)
  end
```

61. The number of comparisons made by this algorithm is related to N, the number of items in the list, as

(A) $O(N)$ (B) $O(2(N−1))$ (C) $O(N\log N)$ (D) $O(N^2)$ (E) $O(N^3)$

62. Which is the strongest of the following asssertions that is satisfied at the point of the segment that is marked (* 1 *) after the conclusion of the inner **for**-loop?

(A) $List[j−1] \geq List[j]$ for all j such that $N − Pass < j \leq N$.
(B) $List[j−1] > List[j]$ for all j such that $N − Pass < j \leq N$.
(C) $List[j−1] > List[j]$ for all j such that $N − Pass \leq j \leq N$.
(D) $List[j] \geq List[j+1]$ for all j such that $1 \leq j \leq N − Pass$.
(E) $List[j] > List[j+1]$ for all j such that $1 < j < N − Pass$.

GO ON TO THE NEXT PAGE.

Q_2Q_1 \ X	0	1
00	01	00
01	10	00
10	11	01
11	01	01

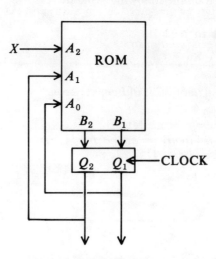

The state table for a controller with a single input X is shown on the left above. It is to be implemented by means of an 8-word by 2-bit, read-only memory (ROM) and a 2-bit register, as shown on the right above. A_2 is the most significant address bit of the ROM. (When X changes, it does so synchronously with the CLOCK, so that it does not cause a race condition.) Which of the following lists the requisite contents of ROM locations 0-7, respectively?

(A) 10 00 10 00 11 01 01 01

(B) 01 10 11 01 00 00 01 01

(C) 01 10 01 11 00 00 01 01

(D) 01 00 10 00 01 01 11 01

(E) 01 00 00 10 11 01 01 01

GO ON TO THE NEXT PAGE.

64. The following program is written in a language having the syntax of Pascal, but one in which passing parameters might not be limited to call by value and call by reference, as in Pascal.

```
program Param(input,output) ;
var
  a,b : integer ;
  procedure p(x,y : integer) ;
  begin
    x := x+2 ;
    a := x*y ;
    x := x+1
  end ;
begin
  a := 1 ;
  b := 2 ;
  p(a,b) ;
  writeln(a)
end.
```

Under which of the following parameter-passing mechanisms will the output of the program be 4 ?

(A) Call by value
(B) Call by reference
(C) Call by name
(D) Call by value-result
(E) None of the above

GO ON TO THE NEXT PAGE.

65. Consider the following algorithm for $n > 0$.

```
const
    n = < some positive integer > ;

var
    a,b,p,Sum : integer ;

begin
    a := 0;   b := n;   Sum := 0 ;
    readln(p) ;
    while a < n  and  b > 0  do
      begin
        if  p > 0   then
          begin
            a := a + 1 ;
            Sum := Sum + 1
          end
        else
          begin
            a := a - 1 ;
            b := b - 1 ;
            Sum := Sum + 1
          end ;
        Modify(p)  { p is called by reference, and Modify }
                   { does not affect the value of any     }
                   { other variable.                      }
      end
end
```

Of the following, which best approximates the largest possible value of *Sum* when the algorithm terminates?

(A) $3n$

(B) $4n$

(C) $5n$

(D) $2n^2$

(E) $3n^2$

GO ON TO THE NEXT PAGE.

66. Which of the following assertions has the property that if the assertion is true before executing the program fragment

$$z := z * a; \; y := y - 1$$

then it will also be true afterward?

(A) $a * y = z$ (B) $z = a^y$ (C) $a^b = z * a^y$ (D) $y > 0 \wedge z = a^k$

(E) None of the above

---

67. A microcomputer used for data acquisition and control is required to digitize and process four analog input signals and to output their average continually; i.e., in real time. The time for an external analog-to-digital converter (which is triggered by a CPU instruction) to digitize one input is 12 microseconds, and only one digitization occurs at a time. Five CPU instructions, including the triggering instruction, must be executed for each signal digitized. Ten CPU instructions are executed in order to average each set of four samples and output this value. The time to convert the output from digital to analog form is to be ignored. If it is assumed that suitable data buffering is employed, then the maximum average instruction execution time that allows the microcomputer to keep up with the input-output data rates, is

(A) 0.8 μs   (B) 1.2 μs   (C) 1.6 μs   (D) 2.4 μs   (E) 3.2 μs

---

GO ON TO THE NEXT PAGE.

68. A programming language L uses the following structure for conditional statements.

> **if** B_1 **then** S_1
>
> B_2 **then** S_2
>
> .
>
> .
>
> .
>
> B_n **then** S_n
>
> **else** S_{n+1}
>
> **endif**
>
> α :

The B_i's are Boolean expressions and the S_i's are (possibly compound) statements. In execution, $B_1, B_2, \ldots$ are tested in turn. If B_i is the first Boolean with value *true*, then S_i is executed and control is passed to the statement labeled α. If all B_i's are false, then S_{n+1} is executed and control is passed to the statement labeled α. In L the conditional structure

> **if** B_1 **then** S_1
>
> $\neg B_2$ **then** S_2
>
> **else** S_3
>
> **endif**

is equivalent to which of the following?

I. **if** B_1 **then** S_1
>   **else if** B_2 **then** S_2
>   **else** S_3

II. **if** $\neg B_1$ **then if** $\neg B_2$ **then** S_2
>   **else** S_3
>   **else** S_1

III. **if** B_1 **then** S_1
>   **else if** $\neg B_2$ **then** S_2
>   **else** S_3

(A) II only   (B) I and II only   (C) I and III only   (D) II and III only   (E) I, II, and III

GO ON TO THE NEXT PAGE.

69. Which of the following regular expressions is equivalent to (describes the same set of strings as) $(a^* + b)^*(c + d)$?

(A) $a^*(c + d) + b(c + d)$

(B) $a^*(c + d)^* + b(c + d)^*$

(C) $a^*(c + d) + b^*(c + d)$

(D) $(a + b)^*c + (a + b)^*d$

(E) $(a^* + b)c + (a^* + b)d$

---

70. A "true-false-zero-one" element is a combinational circuit, whose output depends on a single data input x and two control inputs a and b. The output is 0 or 1 or x or $\bar{x}$, in 1:1 correspondence with the four combinations of a and b. Which of the following Boolean expressions could be used to describe the output of such an element?

I. $ab x \vee \bar{a}\bar{b}\bar{x}$

II. $ax \vee b\bar{x}$

III. $(a \vee x)(\bar{b} \vee \bar{x})$

(A) None　　(B) I only　　(C) II only　　(D) III only　　(E) Either II or III

---

71. An information-retrieval system stores records with 5-bit keys. In response to a given query, which is a 5-bit key q, the system lists all records whose keys k have Hamming distance at most 1 from q; i.e., k and q differ in at most one bit position. Suppose the keys of all the records in the system are:

```
00000
00011
01101
10100
11111
```

In response to an arbitrary query q, what are the minimum and maximum numbers of these records the system could list?

	Minimum	Maximum
(A)	0	2
(B)	0	1
(C)	1	2
(D)	0	3
(E)	1	5

GO ON TO THE NEXT PAGE.

72.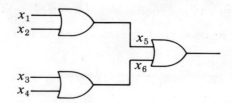

Suppose that one of the three OR-gates in the figure above has a fault, which causes it to behave as if one of its inputs is stuck at 0. For example, if x_2 were stuck at 0, the output of that OR-gate would equal x_1 regardless of the actual value of the signal applied to x_2. If it is known that exactly one of the six inputs, x_1 through x_6, is stuck at 0, what is the minimum number of test vectors (x_1, x_2, x_3, x_4) from which a sequence of tests can always be applied that will uniquely identify which input is stuck at 0 ?

(A) 2   (B) 4   (C) 6   (D) 7   (E) 8

---

73. Let $b_q b_{q-1} \ldots b_0$ be the binary representation of integer b. The integer 3 is a divisor of b if and only if

(A) $b_1 = b_0 = 1$

(B) the sum of the binary digits b_i is divisible by 9

(C) the sum of the binary digits b_i is divisible by 3 but not by 9

(D) the alternating sum $b_0 - b_1 + b_2 - \ldots$ is zero

(E) the alternating sum $b_0 - b_1 + b_2 - \ldots$ is divisible by 3

---

74. Two alternatives for interconnecting a set of processors with bidirectional links are (1) the fully interconnected network, in which each processor is directly connected to every other processor, and (2) the ring network, in which each processor is connected to two other processors. The worst-case path length for a network is the maximum, over all pairs of nodes in the network, of the minimum length paths (measured in number of links) between the nodes. For each type of interconnection of n processors, a figure of merit can be formed as the product of the number of links required for the network times the worst-case path length connecting any two processors. The ratio of this figure of merit for the fully interconnected network compared to that of the ring network, for even $n > 2$, is

(A) $1/(n^2)$ (B) $1/(n(n-1))$ (C) $1/n$ (D) $(n-1)/n$ (E) $(n-1)/(2n)$

GO ON TO THE NEXT PAGE.

Questions 75-76 are based on a complex assembly line of four stages designed with feedback so that a given item can go through a single stage more than once. Two or more stages can act on the item during one time unit. This assembly line is described by the table below, in which an X in row S_i and column t_j indicates that at time t_j, stage S_i is acting on the item that entered the assembly line at time t_0.

	t_0	t_1	t_2	t_3	t_4	t_5	t_6
S_0	X					X	
S_1			X				X
S_2		X		X			
S_3			X		X		

75. If each stage can act on only one item in any time unit, at which time unit(s) between t_1 and t_6 could one introduce a second item into this assembly line?

(A) t_1 only

(B) t_1 or t_3 only

(C) t_1 or t_4 only

(D) t_1 or t_3 or t_6 only

(E) t_1 or t_3 or t_4 or t_6

76. If throughput is to be maximized for the assembly line, at which constant interval, measured in time units, could new items be periodically introduced without violating the time constraints?

(A) 1   (B) 2   (C) 3   (D) 6   (E) 7

GO ON TO THE NEXT PAGE.

77. Which of the following BNF rules is equivalent to

$$P ::= <var>Q$$
$$Q ::= P<op>Q \mid \epsilon$$

where $<var>$ is any variable and $<op>$ is any binary operator?

(A) $P ::= PP<op> \mid <var>$

(B) $P ::= P<op>P \mid <var>$

(C) $P ::= <op>PP \mid <var>$

(D) $P ::= <var>P<op> \mid <var>$

(E) None of the above

Questions 78-79 are based on the table below, which lists eight jobs to be scheduled on two identical processors, the times at which these jobs become available, and their required processing times. Assume that jobs can be scheduled instantly.

Job	Available	Processing Time
A	0	6
B	0	2
C	0	3
D	2	5
E	3	4
F	5	1
G	7	3
H	9	6

78. What is the earliest time at which processing of all jobs can be completed?

(A) 14   (B) 15   (C) 16   (D) 17   (E) 18

79. For the preceding table, assume that the criterion for scheduling is to minimize the delay in starting the processing of each job and assume no preemption. This minimum average delay in starting time is most nearly

(A) 1   (B) 1.25   (C) 1.38   (D) 1.5   (E) 1.75

GO ON TO THE NEXT PAGE.

80. Sam and Sue are using a program P to generate personalized greeting cards on their Cucumber AT micro-computer. Business is so good that they must generate one card every 3 seconds. However, the memory requirements of a run of program P range between 0 and 1,000,000 bytes, distributed uniformly. Further-more, if a run requires r bytes, and the Cucumber's memory is m bytes, then the run takes

    (i)   1 second if $r \leqq m$, and takes

    (ii) r/m seconds if $r > m$, because of byte swapping.

The minimum amount of memory that Sam and Sue must buy so that they can produce an average of one card every 3 seconds is approximately

(A) 172,000 bytes   (B) 333,000 bytes   (C) 484,000 bytes

(D) 732,000 bytes   (E) 889,000 bytes

IF YOU FINISH BEFORE TIME IS CALLED, YOU MAY CHECK YOUR WORK ON THIS TEST.

The Subject Tests are intended to measure your achievement in a specialized field of study. Most of the questions are concerned with subject matter which is probably familiar to you, but some of the questions may refer to areas which you have not studied.

Many examinees wonder whether or not to guess the answers to questions about which they are not certain. In this test a percentage of the wrong answers will be subtracted from the number of right answers as a correction for haphazard guessing. It is improbable, therefore, that mere guessing will improve your score significantly; it may even lower your score, and it does take time. If, however, you are not sure of the correct answer but have some knowledge of the question and are able to eliminate one or more of the answer choices as wrong, your chance of getting the right answer is improved, and on the average it will be to your advantage to answer such a question.

You are advised to use your time effectively and to work as rapidly as you can without losing accuracy. Do not spend too much time on questions that are too difficult for you. Go on to the other questions and come back to the difficult ones later if you can.

YOU ARE TO INDICATE ALL OF YOUR ANSWERS ON THE SEPARATE ANSWER SHEET. No credit will be given for anything written in this examination book. After you have decided which of the suggested answers is correct, blacken the corresponding space on the answer sheet. Be sure to:

- Use a soft black lead pencil (No. 2 or HB).

- Mark <u>only one</u> answer to each question. No credit will be given for multiple answers.

- Mark your answer in the row with the same number as the number of the question you are answering.

- Carefully and completely blacken the space corresponding to the answer you choose for each question. Fill the space with a dark mark so that you cannot see the letter inside the space. Light or partial marks may not be read by the scoring machine. See the example of proper and improper answer marks below.

- Erase all stray marks. If you change an answer, be sure that you completely erase the old answer before marking your new answer. Incomplete erasures may be read as intended answers.

Example:

Sample Answer

What city is the capital of France?

(A) Rome
(B) Paris
(C) London
(D) Cairo
(E) Oslo

Ⓐ ● Ⓒ Ⓓ Ⓔ   CORRECT ANSWER PROPERLY MARKED

Ⓐ Ⓑ Ⓒ Ⓓ Ⓔ
Ⓐ Ⓑ Ⓒ Ⓓ Ⓔ   IMPROPER MARKS
Ⓐ Ⓑ Ⓒ Ⓓ Ⓔ
Ⓐ Ⓑ Ⓒ Ⓓ Ⓔ

Do not be concerned that the answer sheet provides spaces for more answers than there are questions in this test.

CLOSE YOUR TEST BOOK AND WAIT FOR FURTHER INSTRUCTIONS FROM THE SUPERVISOR.

The Committee of Examiners for the Computer Science Test of the Graduate Record Examinations, appointed with the advice of the Association for Computing Machinery and the IEEE Computer Society:

Michael Faiman, University of Illinois at Urbana-Champaign, Chairman
Alan Demers, Cornell University
Edward Lazowska, University of Washington
Martha Sloan, Michigan Technological University
Jeffrey Ullman, Stanford University

with the assistance of

J. R. Jefferson Wadkins, Educational Testing Service
Steven Anacker, Educational Testing Service

I

NOTE: To ensure the prompt and accurate processing of test results, your cooperation in following these directions is needed. The procedures that follow have been kept to the minimum necessary. They will take a few minutes to complete, but it is essential that you fill in all blanks exactly as directed.

SUBJECT TEST

A. Print and sign your full name in this box:

PRINT: _____
          (LAST)   (FIRST)   (MIDDLE)

SIGN: _____

B. Your answer sheet contains areas which will be used to ensure accurate reporting of your test results. It is essential that you fill in these areas exactly as explained below.

1. YOUR NAME, MAILING ADDRESS, AND TEST CENTER: Place your answer sheet so that the heading "Graduate Record Examinations—Subject Test" is at the top. In box 1 below that heading print your name. Enter your current mailing address. Print the name of the city, state or province, and country in which the test center is located, and the center number.

2. YOUR NAME: Print all the information requested in the boxes at the top of the columns (first four letters of your last name, your first initial, and middle initial), and then blacken fully the appropriate space beneath each entry.

3. DATE OF BIRTH: Blacken the space beside the month in which you were born. Then enter the day of the month on which you were born in the boxes at the top of the columns. Blacken the appropriate space beneath each entry. Be sure to treat zeros like any other digit, and to add a zero before any single digit; for example 03, not 3. (Your year of birth is not required on the answer sheet.)

4. SEX: Blacken the appropriate space.

5. REGISTRATION NUMBER: Copy your registration number from your admission ticket into the boxes at the top of the columns and then blacken the appropriate space beneath each entry. Check your admission ticket again to make certain that you have copied your registration number accurately.

6. TITLE CODE: Copy the numbers shown below and blacken the appropriate spaces beneath each entry as shown. When you have completed item 6, check to be sure it is identical to the illustration below.

7. CERTIFICATION STATEMENT: In the boxed area, please write (do not print) the following statement: I certify that I am the person whose name appears on this answer sheet. I also agree not to disclose the contents of the test I am taking today to anyone. Sign and date where indicated.

8. TEST NAME: Copy _Computer Science_
   FORM CODE: Copy ____GR 8629____

9. TEST BOOK SERIAL NUMBER: Copy the serial number of your test book in the box. It is printed in red at the upper right on the front cover of your test book.

C. WHEN YOU HAVE FINISHED THESE INSTRUCTIONS, PLEASE TURN YOUR ANSWER SHEET OVER AND SIGN YOUR NAME IN THE BOX EXACTLY AS YOU DID FOR ITEM 7.

When you have finished, wait for further instructions from the supervisor. DO NOT OPEN YOUR TEST BOOK UNTIL YOU ARE TOLD TO DO SO.

GRADUATE RECORD EXAMINATIONS
SUBJECT TEST

Use only a pencil with a soft, black lead (No. 2 or HB) to complete this answer sheet. Be sure to fill in completely the space that corresponds to your answer choice. Completely erase any errors or stray marks.

SIDE 1

1.

YOUR NAME: _____
(PRINT)   Last Name (Family or Surname)   First Name (Given)   M.I.

MAILING ADDRESS: _____
(PRINT)   P.O. Box or Street Address

City   State or Province   Country   Zip or Postal Code

CENTER: _____
(PRINT)   City   State or Province   Country   Center Number

2. YOUR NAME

First 4 letters of last name				First Init.	Mid. Init.

(A through Z bubbles, plus dash bubble for first 4 letters columns)

3. DATE OF BIRTH

Month	Day
○ Jan.	
○ Feb.	
○ Mar.	
○ Apr.	
○ May	
○ June	
○ July	
○ Aug.	
○ Sept.	
○ Oct.	
○ Nov.	
○ Dec.	

4. SEX ○ Male ○ Female

SHADED AREA FOR ETS USE ONLY

5. REGISTRATION NUMBER

6. TITLE CODE

(Bubble columns 0–9)

7. CERTIFICATION STATEMENT

_____
_____
_____
_____
_____
_____

SIGNATURE: _____   DATE: ___/___/___
Mo. Day Year

8.
TEST NAME: _____

FORM CODE: _____

9. TEST BOOK SERIAL NUMBER

BE SURE EACH MARK IS DARK AND COMPLETELY FILLS THE INTENDED SPACE AS ILLUSTRATED HERE: ●.
YOU MAY FIND MORE RESPONSE SPACES THAN YOU NEED. IF SO, PLEASE LEAVE THEM BLANK.

1 Ⓐ Ⓑ Ⓒ Ⓓ Ⓔ	17 Ⓐ Ⓑ Ⓒ Ⓓ Ⓔ	33 Ⓐ Ⓑ Ⓒ Ⓓ Ⓔ	49 Ⓐ Ⓑ Ⓒ Ⓓ Ⓔ	65 Ⓐ Ⓑ Ⓒ Ⓓ Ⓔ
2 Ⓐ Ⓑ Ⓒ Ⓓ Ⓔ	18 Ⓐ Ⓑ Ⓒ Ⓓ Ⓔ	34 Ⓐ Ⓑ Ⓒ Ⓓ Ⓔ	50 Ⓐ Ⓑ Ⓒ Ⓓ Ⓔ	66 Ⓐ Ⓑ Ⓒ Ⓓ Ⓔ
3 Ⓐ Ⓑ Ⓒ Ⓓ Ⓔ	19 Ⓐ Ⓑ Ⓒ Ⓓ Ⓔ	35 Ⓐ Ⓑ Ⓒ Ⓓ Ⓔ	51 Ⓐ Ⓑ Ⓒ Ⓓ Ⓔ	67 Ⓐ Ⓑ Ⓒ Ⓓ Ⓔ
4 Ⓐ Ⓑ Ⓒ Ⓓ Ⓔ	20 Ⓐ Ⓑ Ⓒ Ⓓ Ⓔ	36 Ⓐ Ⓑ Ⓒ Ⓓ Ⓔ	52 Ⓐ Ⓑ Ⓒ Ⓓ Ⓔ	68 Ⓐ Ⓑ Ⓒ Ⓓ Ⓔ
5 Ⓐ Ⓑ Ⓒ Ⓓ Ⓔ	21 Ⓐ Ⓑ Ⓒ Ⓓ Ⓔ	37 Ⓐ Ⓑ Ⓒ Ⓓ Ⓔ	53 Ⓐ Ⓑ Ⓒ Ⓓ Ⓔ	69 Ⓐ Ⓑ Ⓒ Ⓓ Ⓔ
6 Ⓐ Ⓑ Ⓒ Ⓓ Ⓔ	22 Ⓐ Ⓑ Ⓒ Ⓓ Ⓔ	38 Ⓐ Ⓑ Ⓒ Ⓓ Ⓔ	54 Ⓐ Ⓑ Ⓒ Ⓓ Ⓔ	70 Ⓐ Ⓑ Ⓒ Ⓓ Ⓔ
7 Ⓐ Ⓑ Ⓒ Ⓓ Ⓔ	23 Ⓐ Ⓑ Ⓒ Ⓓ Ⓔ	39 Ⓐ Ⓑ Ⓒ Ⓓ Ⓔ	55 Ⓐ Ⓑ Ⓒ Ⓓ Ⓔ	71 Ⓐ Ⓑ Ⓒ Ⓓ Ⓔ
8 Ⓐ Ⓑ Ⓒ Ⓓ Ⓔ	24 Ⓐ Ⓑ Ⓒ Ⓓ Ⓔ	40 Ⓐ Ⓑ Ⓒ Ⓓ Ⓔ	56 Ⓐ Ⓑ Ⓒ Ⓓ Ⓔ	72 Ⓐ Ⓑ Ⓒ Ⓓ Ⓔ
9 Ⓐ Ⓑ Ⓒ Ⓓ Ⓔ	25 Ⓐ Ⓑ Ⓒ Ⓓ Ⓔ	41 Ⓐ Ⓑ Ⓒ Ⓓ Ⓔ	57 Ⓐ Ⓑ Ⓒ Ⓓ Ⓔ	73 Ⓐ Ⓑ Ⓒ Ⓓ Ⓔ
10 Ⓐ Ⓑ Ⓒ Ⓓ Ⓔ	26 Ⓐ Ⓑ Ⓒ Ⓓ Ⓔ	42 Ⓐ Ⓑ Ⓒ Ⓓ Ⓔ	58 Ⓐ Ⓑ Ⓒ Ⓓ Ⓔ	74 Ⓐ Ⓑ Ⓒ Ⓓ Ⓔ
11 Ⓐ Ⓑ Ⓒ Ⓓ Ⓔ	27 Ⓐ Ⓑ Ⓒ Ⓓ Ⓔ	43 Ⓐ Ⓑ Ⓒ Ⓓ Ⓔ	59 Ⓐ Ⓑ Ⓒ Ⓓ Ⓔ	75 Ⓐ Ⓑ Ⓒ Ⓓ Ⓔ
12 Ⓐ Ⓑ Ⓒ Ⓓ Ⓔ	28 Ⓐ Ⓑ Ⓒ Ⓓ Ⓔ	44 Ⓐ Ⓑ Ⓒ Ⓓ Ⓔ	60 Ⓐ Ⓑ Ⓒ Ⓓ Ⓔ	76 Ⓐ Ⓑ Ⓒ Ⓓ Ⓔ
13 Ⓐ Ⓑ Ⓒ Ⓓ Ⓔ	29 Ⓐ Ⓑ Ⓒ Ⓓ Ⓔ	45 Ⓐ Ⓑ Ⓒ Ⓓ Ⓔ	61 Ⓐ Ⓑ Ⓒ Ⓓ Ⓔ	77 Ⓐ Ⓑ Ⓒ Ⓓ Ⓔ
14 Ⓐ Ⓑ Ⓒ Ⓓ Ⓔ	30 Ⓐ Ⓑ Ⓒ Ⓓ Ⓔ	46 Ⓐ Ⓑ Ⓒ Ⓓ Ⓔ	62 Ⓐ Ⓑ Ⓒ Ⓓ Ⓔ	78 Ⓐ Ⓑ Ⓒ Ⓓ Ⓔ
15 Ⓐ Ⓑ Ⓒ Ⓓ Ⓔ	31 Ⓐ Ⓑ Ⓒ Ⓓ Ⓔ	47 Ⓐ Ⓑ Ⓒ Ⓓ Ⓔ	63 Ⓐ Ⓑ Ⓒ Ⓓ Ⓔ	79 Ⓐ Ⓑ Ⓒ Ⓓ Ⓔ
16 Ⓐ Ⓑ Ⓒ Ⓓ Ⓔ	32 Ⓐ Ⓑ Ⓒ Ⓓ Ⓔ	48 Ⓐ Ⓑ Ⓒ Ⓓ Ⓔ	64 Ⓐ Ⓑ Ⓒ Ⓓ Ⓔ	80 Ⓐ Ⓑ Ⓒ Ⓓ Ⓔ

Item responses continued on reverse side.

SIGNATURE:

Use only a pencil with a soft, black lead (No. 2 or HB) to complete this answer sheet. Be sure to fill in completely the space that corresponds to your answer choice. Completely erase any errors or stray marks.

YOU MAY FIND MORE RESPONSE SPACES THAN YOU NEED. IF SO, PLEASE LEAVE THEM BLANK.

TURN
ANSWER
SHEET
OVER
AND
BEGIN
TEST
ON
SIDE 1.

81 Ⓐ Ⓑ Ⓒ Ⓓ Ⓔ	121 Ⓐ Ⓑ Ⓒ Ⓓ Ⓔ	161 Ⓐ Ⓑ Ⓒ Ⓓ Ⓔ	201 Ⓐ Ⓑ Ⓒ Ⓓ Ⓔ
82 Ⓐ Ⓑ Ⓒ Ⓓ Ⓔ	122 Ⓐ Ⓑ Ⓒ Ⓓ Ⓔ	162 Ⓐ Ⓑ Ⓒ Ⓓ Ⓔ	202 Ⓐ Ⓑ Ⓒ Ⓓ Ⓔ
83 Ⓐ Ⓑ Ⓒ Ⓓ Ⓔ	123 Ⓐ Ⓑ Ⓒ Ⓓ Ⓔ	163 Ⓐ Ⓑ Ⓒ Ⓓ Ⓔ	203 Ⓐ Ⓑ Ⓒ Ⓓ Ⓔ
84 Ⓐ Ⓑ Ⓒ Ⓓ Ⓔ	124 Ⓐ Ⓑ Ⓒ Ⓓ Ⓔ	164 Ⓐ Ⓑ Ⓒ Ⓓ Ⓔ	204 Ⓐ Ⓑ Ⓒ Ⓓ Ⓔ
85 Ⓐ Ⓑ Ⓒ Ⓓ Ⓔ	125 Ⓐ Ⓑ Ⓒ Ⓓ Ⓔ	165 Ⓐ Ⓑ Ⓒ Ⓓ Ⓔ	205 Ⓐ Ⓑ Ⓒ Ⓓ Ⓔ
86 Ⓐ Ⓑ Ⓒ Ⓓ Ⓔ	126 Ⓐ Ⓑ Ⓒ Ⓓ Ⓔ	166 Ⓐ Ⓑ Ⓒ Ⓓ Ⓔ	206 Ⓐ Ⓑ Ⓒ Ⓓ Ⓔ
87 Ⓐ Ⓑ Ⓒ Ⓓ Ⓔ	127 Ⓐ Ⓑ Ⓒ Ⓓ Ⓔ	167 Ⓐ Ⓑ Ⓒ Ⓓ Ⓔ	207 Ⓐ Ⓑ Ⓒ Ⓓ Ⓔ
88 Ⓐ Ⓑ Ⓒ Ⓓ Ⓔ	128 Ⓐ Ⓑ Ⓒ Ⓓ Ⓔ	168 Ⓐ Ⓑ Ⓒ Ⓓ Ⓔ	208 Ⓐ Ⓑ Ⓒ Ⓓ Ⓔ
89 Ⓐ Ⓑ Ⓒ Ⓓ Ⓔ	129 Ⓐ Ⓑ Ⓒ Ⓓ Ⓔ	169 Ⓐ Ⓑ Ⓒ Ⓓ Ⓔ	209 Ⓐ Ⓑ Ⓒ Ⓓ Ⓔ
90 Ⓐ Ⓑ Ⓒ Ⓓ Ⓔ	130 Ⓐ Ⓑ Ⓒ Ⓓ Ⓔ	170 Ⓐ Ⓑ Ⓒ Ⓓ Ⓔ	210 Ⓐ Ⓑ Ⓒ Ⓓ Ⓔ
91 Ⓐ Ⓑ Ⓒ Ⓓ Ⓔ	131 Ⓐ Ⓑ Ⓒ Ⓓ Ⓔ	171 Ⓐ Ⓑ Ⓒ Ⓓ Ⓔ	211 Ⓐ Ⓑ Ⓒ Ⓓ Ⓔ
92 Ⓐ Ⓑ Ⓒ Ⓓ Ⓔ	132 Ⓐ Ⓑ Ⓒ Ⓓ Ⓔ	172 Ⓐ Ⓑ Ⓒ Ⓓ Ⓔ	212 Ⓐ Ⓑ Ⓒ Ⓓ Ⓔ
93 Ⓐ Ⓑ Ⓒ Ⓓ Ⓔ	133 Ⓐ Ⓑ Ⓒ Ⓓ Ⓔ	173 Ⓐ Ⓑ Ⓒ Ⓓ Ⓔ	213 Ⓐ Ⓑ Ⓒ Ⓓ Ⓔ
94 Ⓐ Ⓑ Ⓒ Ⓓ Ⓔ	134 Ⓐ Ⓑ Ⓒ Ⓓ Ⓔ	174 Ⓐ Ⓑ Ⓒ Ⓓ Ⓔ	214 Ⓐ Ⓑ Ⓒ Ⓓ Ⓔ
95 Ⓐ Ⓑ Ⓒ Ⓓ Ⓔ	135 Ⓐ Ⓑ Ⓒ Ⓓ Ⓔ	175 Ⓐ Ⓑ Ⓒ Ⓓ Ⓔ	215 Ⓐ Ⓑ Ⓒ Ⓓ Ⓔ
96 Ⓐ Ⓑ Ⓒ Ⓓ Ⓔ	136 Ⓐ Ⓑ Ⓒ Ⓓ Ⓔ	176 Ⓐ Ⓑ Ⓒ Ⓓ Ⓔ	216 Ⓐ Ⓑ Ⓒ Ⓓ Ⓔ
97 Ⓐ Ⓑ Ⓒ Ⓓ Ⓔ	137 Ⓐ Ⓑ Ⓒ Ⓓ Ⓔ	177 Ⓐ Ⓑ Ⓒ Ⓓ Ⓔ	217 Ⓐ Ⓑ Ⓒ Ⓓ Ⓔ
98 Ⓐ Ⓑ Ⓒ Ⓓ Ⓔ	138 Ⓐ Ⓑ Ⓒ Ⓓ Ⓔ	178 Ⓐ Ⓑ Ⓒ Ⓓ Ⓔ	218 Ⓐ Ⓑ Ⓒ Ⓓ Ⓔ
99 Ⓐ Ⓑ Ⓒ Ⓓ Ⓔ	139 Ⓐ Ⓑ Ⓒ Ⓓ Ⓔ	179 Ⓐ Ⓑ Ⓒ Ⓓ Ⓔ	219 Ⓐ Ⓑ Ⓒ Ⓓ Ⓔ
100 Ⓐ Ⓑ Ⓒ Ⓓ Ⓔ	140 Ⓐ Ⓑ Ⓒ Ⓓ Ⓔ	180 Ⓐ Ⓑ Ⓒ Ⓓ Ⓔ	220 Ⓐ Ⓑ Ⓒ Ⓓ Ⓔ
101 Ⓐ Ⓑ Ⓒ Ⓓ Ⓔ	141 Ⓐ Ⓑ Ⓒ Ⓓ Ⓔ	181 Ⓐ Ⓑ Ⓒ Ⓓ Ⓔ	221 Ⓐ Ⓑ Ⓒ Ⓓ Ⓔ
102 Ⓐ Ⓑ Ⓒ Ⓓ Ⓔ	142 Ⓐ Ⓑ Ⓒ Ⓓ Ⓔ	182 Ⓐ Ⓑ Ⓒ Ⓓ Ⓔ	222 Ⓐ Ⓑ Ⓒ Ⓓ Ⓔ
103 Ⓐ Ⓑ Ⓒ Ⓓ Ⓔ	143 Ⓐ Ⓑ Ⓒ Ⓓ Ⓔ	183 Ⓐ Ⓑ Ⓒ Ⓓ Ⓔ	223 Ⓐ Ⓑ Ⓒ Ⓓ Ⓔ
104 Ⓐ Ⓑ Ⓒ Ⓓ Ⓔ	144 Ⓐ Ⓑ Ⓒ Ⓓ Ⓔ	184 Ⓐ Ⓑ Ⓒ Ⓓ Ⓔ	224 Ⓐ Ⓑ Ⓒ Ⓓ Ⓔ
105 Ⓐ Ⓑ Ⓒ Ⓓ Ⓔ	145 Ⓐ Ⓑ Ⓒ Ⓓ Ⓔ	185 Ⓐ Ⓑ Ⓒ Ⓓ Ⓔ	225 Ⓐ Ⓑ Ⓒ Ⓓ Ⓔ
106 Ⓐ Ⓑ Ⓒ Ⓓ Ⓔ	146 Ⓐ Ⓑ Ⓒ Ⓓ Ⓔ	186 Ⓐ Ⓑ Ⓒ Ⓓ Ⓔ	226 Ⓐ Ⓑ Ⓒ Ⓓ Ⓔ
107 Ⓐ Ⓑ Ⓒ Ⓓ Ⓔ	147 Ⓐ Ⓑ Ⓒ Ⓓ Ⓔ	187 Ⓐ Ⓑ Ⓒ Ⓓ Ⓔ	227 Ⓐ Ⓑ Ⓒ Ⓓ Ⓔ
108 Ⓐ Ⓑ Ⓒ Ⓓ Ⓔ	148 Ⓐ Ⓑ Ⓒ Ⓓ Ⓔ	188 Ⓐ Ⓑ Ⓒ Ⓓ Ⓔ	228 Ⓐ Ⓑ Ⓒ Ⓓ Ⓔ
109 Ⓐ Ⓑ Ⓒ Ⓓ Ⓔ	149 Ⓐ Ⓑ Ⓒ Ⓓ Ⓔ	189 Ⓐ Ⓑ Ⓒ Ⓓ Ⓔ	229 Ⓐ Ⓑ Ⓒ Ⓓ Ⓔ
110 Ⓐ Ⓑ Ⓒ Ⓓ Ⓔ	150 Ⓐ Ⓑ Ⓒ Ⓓ Ⓔ	190 Ⓐ Ⓑ Ⓒ Ⓓ Ⓔ	230 Ⓐ Ⓑ Ⓒ Ⓓ Ⓔ
111 Ⓐ Ⓑ Ⓒ Ⓓ Ⓔ	151 Ⓐ Ⓑ Ⓒ Ⓓ Ⓔ	191 Ⓐ Ⓑ Ⓒ Ⓓ Ⓔ	231 Ⓐ Ⓑ Ⓒ Ⓓ Ⓔ
112 Ⓐ Ⓑ Ⓒ Ⓓ Ⓔ	152 Ⓐ Ⓑ Ⓒ Ⓓ Ⓔ	192 Ⓐ Ⓑ Ⓒ Ⓓ Ⓔ	232 Ⓐ Ⓑ Ⓒ Ⓓ Ⓔ
113 Ⓐ Ⓑ Ⓒ Ⓓ Ⓔ	153 Ⓐ Ⓑ Ⓒ Ⓓ Ⓔ	193 Ⓐ Ⓑ Ⓒ Ⓓ Ⓔ	233 Ⓐ Ⓑ Ⓒ Ⓓ Ⓔ
114 Ⓐ Ⓑ Ⓒ Ⓓ Ⓔ	154 Ⓐ Ⓑ Ⓒ Ⓓ Ⓔ	194 Ⓐ Ⓑ Ⓒ Ⓓ Ⓔ	234 Ⓐ Ⓑ Ⓒ Ⓓ Ⓔ
115 Ⓐ Ⓑ Ⓒ Ⓓ Ⓔ	155 Ⓐ Ⓑ Ⓒ Ⓓ Ⓔ	195 Ⓐ Ⓑ Ⓒ Ⓓ Ⓔ	235 Ⓐ Ⓑ Ⓒ Ⓓ Ⓔ
116 Ⓐ Ⓑ Ⓒ Ⓓ Ⓔ	156 Ⓐ Ⓑ Ⓒ Ⓓ Ⓔ	196 Ⓐ Ⓑ Ⓒ Ⓓ Ⓔ	236 Ⓐ Ⓑ Ⓒ Ⓓ Ⓔ
117 Ⓐ Ⓑ Ⓒ Ⓓ Ⓔ	157 Ⓐ Ⓑ Ⓒ Ⓓ Ⓔ	197 Ⓐ Ⓑ Ⓒ Ⓓ Ⓔ	237 Ⓐ Ⓑ Ⓒ Ⓓ Ⓔ
118 Ⓐ Ⓑ Ⓒ Ⓓ Ⓔ	158 Ⓐ Ⓑ Ⓒ Ⓓ Ⓔ	198 Ⓐ Ⓑ Ⓒ Ⓓ Ⓔ	238 Ⓐ Ⓑ Ⓒ Ⓓ Ⓔ
119 Ⓐ Ⓑ Ⓒ Ⓓ Ⓔ	159 Ⓐ Ⓑ Ⓒ Ⓓ Ⓔ	199 Ⓐ Ⓑ Ⓒ Ⓓ Ⓔ	239 Ⓐ Ⓑ Ⓒ Ⓓ Ⓔ
120 Ⓐ Ⓑ Ⓒ Ⓓ Ⓔ	160 Ⓐ Ⓑ Ⓒ Ⓓ Ⓔ	200 Ⓐ Ⓑ Ⓒ Ⓓ Ⓔ	240 Ⓐ Ⓑ Ⓒ Ⓓ Ⓔ

FOR ETS USE ONLY	TR	TW	TFS	TCS	1R	1W	1FS	1CS	2R	2W	2FS	2CS	3R	3W	3FS	3CS

GRE® PUBLICATIONS ORDER FORM

Graduate Record Examinations
Educational Testing Service
CN 6014
Princeton, NJ 08541-6014

Please send me the publications indicated below.

Catalog Number	Publication	Cover Price	Your Price	No. of Copies	Amount	Postage*	Total
	Directory of Graduate Programs (540-97)						
252012	Volume A—Agriculture, Biological Sciences, Psychology, Health Sciences, and Home Economics	$14.95	$10.00				
252013	Volume B—Arts and Humanities	14.95	10.00				
252014	Volume C—Physical Sciences, Mathematics, and Engineering	14.95	10.00				
252015	Volume D—Social Sciences and Education	14.95	10.00				
	Practice Test Books (540-01)						
241216	Practicing to Take the GRE General Test—No. 4	7.95	7.00				
241215	Practicing to Take the GRE General Test—No. 3	7.95	7.00				
241223	Practicing to Take the GRE Biology Test	6.95	6.00				
241224	Practicing to Take the GRE Chemistry Test	6.95	6.00				
241217	Practicing to Take the GRE Computer Science Test	6.95	6.00				
241218	Practicing to Take the GRE Economics Test	6.95	6.00				
241211	Practicing to Take the GRE Education Test	6.95	6.00				
241221	Practicing to Take the GRE Engineering Test	6.95	6.00				
241219	Practicing to Take the GRE History Test	6.95	6.00				
241225	Practicing to Take the GRE Literature in English Test	6.95	6.00				
241220	Practicing to Take the GRE Physics Test	6.95	6.00				
241222	Practicing to Take the GRE Psychology Test	6.95	6.00				
	Software Editions (540-02)						
299625	Practicing to Take the GRE General Test–Apple Macintosh Software Edition		55.00				
299626	Practicing to Take the GRE General Test–IBM Software Edition		55.00				

*For postage and handling to a single address in North America, U.S. Possessions, or APO addresses, add $3 for the first book ordered and $1 for each additional book. Add $5 per set for each software edition ordered.

To all other locations (by airmail only) to a single address, add $12 for each General Test practice book or software edition ordered and $6 for each Subject Test practice book, add $17 for the first volume of the *Directory of Graduate Programs* ordered, and $1 for each additional volume.

Orders from individuals must be accompanied by payment in full, including postage and handling fee. Payment should be made by check or money order drawn on a bank in the United States or by U.S. Postal Money Order, UNESCO Coupons, or International Postal Reply Coupons.

Orders from individuals received without payment will be returned.

⬆ **Total** ⬆
Amount Due

For ETS
Use (540-52)

DO NOT DETACH THESE MAILING LABELS. PLEASE TYPE OR PRINT CLEARLY BELOW.

Graduate Record Examinations
Educational Testing Service
CN 6014
Princeton, NJ 08541-6014

TO _____

_____

_____

_____

Graduate Record Examinations
Educational Testing Service
CN 6014
Princeton, NJ 08541-6014

TO _____

_____

_____

_____